THE AUDUBON SOCIETY

FIELD GUIDE

to the

BALD
EAGLE

David G. Gordon

SASQUATCH BOOKS
Seattle, Washington

Printed in the United States of America

Third printing 1996

Cover design and illustration: Dugald Stermer
Text illustrations: ©1991 Fred Thomas
Back cover photo: F. Stuart Westmorland
Maps: Karen Schober
Composition: Scribe Typography
Eagle-watching site data compiled by Edie Neeson

International Standard Book Number: 0-912365-46-3

Published by Sasquatch Books
1008 Western Avenue
Seattle, Washington 98104
(206)467-4300

Other titles in the Sasquatch Field Guide series:

People for Puget Sound
Field Guide to the Geoduck

The Western Society of Malacologists
Field Guide to the Slug

The Oceanic Society
Field Guide to the Gray Whale

American Cetacean Society
Field Guide to the Orca

International Society of Cryptozoology
Field Guide to the Sasquatch

Great Bear Foundation
Field Guide to the Grizzly Bear

Adopt-a-Stream Foundation
Field Guide to the Pacific Salmon

Oceanic Society Expeditions/Earthtrust
Field Guide to the Humpback Whale

Contents

Introduction

In the days before European settlement, hundreds of thousands of bald eagles thrived in the United States and Canada. Today, however, the once-plentiful population has dwindled to fewer than 3,000 nesting pairs in the lower 48 states. The territory covered in this book is now a key bald eagle sanctuary. Its rugged coastline, rivers rich with spawning salmon, and dense expanses of evergreen forest provide ideal habitat for this exceptional bird.

Writing a field guide to an endangered animal is a challenge, a constant balancing act between saying too much and saying too little. Bald eagles, like most birds of prey, value their privacy. With this book in hand, nature lovers will be able to find the eagles' major gathering places, primarily well-established wintering areas where human intrusion is least likely to have a harmful effect on the birds. As for nest sites, to prevent harm to future generations of eagles, the locations of most of these precious aeries are best left unidentified.

Being able to understand and appreciate the ways of bald eagles is as important as locating individual birds. For this reason, I've tried to devote ample space to describing facets of the bald eagle's natural history that are least easily observed. For help with these sections, I'm most grateful to a handful of field biologists (and one in particular, Mark Stalmaster) whose works have alerted me to many otherwise inaccessible features of bald eagle life. A special thanks goes to the National Audubon Society, which provided expert reviewers for my manuscript: Alexander Sprunt IV, Jim Pissot, and Randy Snodgrass.

Partial proceeds from the sale of this book help support the National Audubon Society, which provides leadership in scientific research, conservation education, and citizen action programs to save birds and other wildlife and the habitat necessary for their survival.

David G. Gordon

A Word About Bald Eagles

PHYLUM: Chordata (all animals with backbones)

SUBPHYLUM: Vertebrata (animals with developed backbones and other advanced structures)

CLASS: Aves (all birds)

ORDER: Falconiformes (diurnal birds of prey)

FAMILY: Accipitridae (hawks, Old World vultures, and harriers)

GENUS: *Haliaeetus* (Latin for "sea eagle")

SPECIES: *leucocephalus* (Greek for "white-headed")

Within the class Aves, the catchall term "birds of prey" (or "raptors") lumps together more than 400 species. These species can differ considerably in form and behavior, but all share a common characteristic—the ability to hunt and kill live, red-blooded prey. While some birds of prey—owls, for example —are nocturnal, or nighttime, hunters, the vast majority of these highly evolved feathered predators are diurnal, or daytime, hunters.

Eagles and their relatives—hawks, kites, and vultures—are members of the order Falconiformes. Within this order are five families. One of them, the Accipitridae, to which the bald eagle belongs, contains over 200 species of birds. All of these species probably evolved over millions of years from the same basic ancestor, the prehistoric kite of Asia and Australasia.

Familiar North American Accipitridae include the red-tailed hawk, the harrier (also called the marsh hawk), the osprey, and the golden eagle. Although the latter two birds resemble the bald eagle in many ways (in fact, it can be difficult to distinguish an immature bald eagle from an adult golden eagle), neither ospreys nor golden eagles are very closely related to bald eagles.

BALD EAGLE
FAMILY: ACCIPITRIDAE

GOLDEN EAGLE
FAMILY: ACCIPITRIDAE

RED·TAILED HAWK
FAMILY: ACCIPITRIDAE

PEREGRINE FALCON
FAMILY: FALCONIDAE

OSPREY
FAMILY: ACCIPITRIDAE
SUB·FAMILY: PANDIONIDAE

TURKEY VULTURE
FAMILY: CATHARTIDAE

BARN OWL,
ORDER: STRIGIFORMES
FAMILY: TYTONIDAE

BIRDS OF PREY

Closer relatives to the bald eagle are the six other members of the genus *Haliaeetus*, or sea eagles. Sea eagles inhabit the areas around seacoasts, large rivers, and lakes throughout the world. They are powerful birds with large, hooked beaks, unfeathered legs, and sharp talons designed for securing prey. Most are adept at scavenging, hunting, and—when the opportunity arises—pirating food from other bird species.

The bald eagle is the only resident sea eagle in the United States. Some scientists identify two separate subspecies of this bird: a northern race, *Haliaeetus leucocephalus alascanus*; and a southern race, *Haliaeetus leucocephalus leucocephalus*. The sole physical difference between the two is size; the southern subspecies is smaller and lighter than the northern one. However, the difference in size is less obvious midway between the two subspecies' territories. The two subspecies' geographic boundaries are also fairly arbitrary, as their migratory routes overlap, making their territories indistinguishable at times. For these reasons, the notion of two subspecies has been disputed by members of the scientific community.

Bald Eagle Facts

NAME   *Haliaeetus leucocephalus* (Latin and Greek for "white-headed sea eagle"). The bald eagle received its common name from North American colonists at a time when "bald" (or "balled") meant white, not hairless.

LIFE SPAN   Unknown. Two captive bald eagles have lived to 47 years; the life span of a free-flying bald eagle is probably much shorter. Victims of habitat destruction and natural selection, many wild eagles die at a fairly early age.

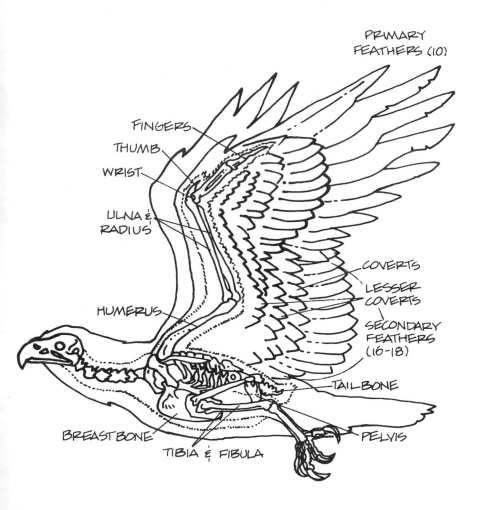

PRIMARY
FEATHERS (10)

FINGERS

THUMB

WRIST

ULNA &
RADIUS

HUMERUS

COVERTS

LESSER
COVERTS

SECONDARY
FEATHERS
(16-18)

TAILBONE

BREASTBONE

TIBIA & FIBULA

PELVIS

From 50 to 70 percent of juveniles die within their first year. As many as 90 percent perish before attaining adult plumage.

SIZE One of the larger members of the family Accipitridae. As with most birds of prey, females are larger than males. Size and weight are also influenced by age and geographic location. In the northwestern United States and western Canada, adult females can reach body lengths of 43 inches (1.1 m), weights of 15 pounds (6.8 kg), and wingspans of 92 inches (2.3 m). Adult males grow to an average body length of 33 inches (.8 m), weight of 9.5 pounds (4.3 kg), and wingspan of 81.6 inches (2.1 m).

COLORATION Changes gradually over the first five years of the eagle's life. Immature: dusky brown head and tail, brownish bill, and blotches of white or cream on body and wings. Adult: snow white head and tail, yellow bill, brownish black body.

VOICE Four different calls have been distinguished. The most common is a high, whining, gull–like scream, broken into a rapid series of notes. Bald eagles are most vocal when threatened, annoyed, or mating.

MATING Fertilization occurs on or near the nest, when the male steps briefly onto the back of the female; the female raises her tail and the male lowers his to make genital contact.

EGGS Clutch consists of one to three (usually two) dull white eggs, usually laid two to four days apart. Incubation is 31 to 36 days.

BROOD Not all eggs hatch: typical brood size is smaller than clutch size, and rarely do nests contain three eaglets. Fledglings leave the nest 72 to 75 days after hatching.

FOOD Scavengers as well as skilled hunters, bald eagles eat nearly anything of nutritional value. Fish are the prey most frequently taken, followed by waterfowl, then small and large mammals. Scavenged meals include winter kills of deer and elk, carcasses of spawning salmon, and remains of stranded whales and dolphins.

DISTRIBUTION Once widespread in North America, now most abundant in Alaska, Canada, Washington, Oregon, northern California, the Great Lakes region, and Florida. Currently classified as endangered and threatened under the federal Endangered Species Act.

The Life of Bald Eagles: Pairing Off

Bald eagles are monogamous, that is, two adults will remain together in a "pair-bond" equivalent to marriage, quite possibly for life. Even if the pair-bond is permanent, however, as many scientists suggest, a bald eagle will mate with another after the death of its mate. Reports by field observers in the Midwest describe one particular female bald eagle who may have had as many as four mates over the course of her lifetime.

No one knows when, where, or how pair-bonding takes place. Bonds may be formed before the breeding season, when eagles socialize in wintering grounds, during the migrations between wintering and breeding grounds, or later on the breeding grounds. All we know for sure is that in late winter or early spring, the skies above favored nesting areas are filled with soaring bald eagle pairs. Accompanied by numerous individual subadults (immature eagles), these seasonal gatherings can occupy several square miles of air space.

A bald eagle pair usually builds a new nest or enlarges its old one in the same general locale for many years in a row. Once a pair has established its territory, the birds are reluctant to breed elsewhere, even when all suitable nest trees have been blown down by wind or felled. Some pairs will remain at such a site for a season or more without breeding, rather than relocate their nests.

The unwillingness of many bald eagles to establish new nest sites is easily understood: finding fresh, unoccupied territory in which to build a nest is no easy chore, and human encroachment is reducing available habitat. In a bid to monopolize the local food and habitat resources, a pair of bald eagles will defend an area around its nest site that may extend up to half a mile (.8 km) in all directions.

Often, an eagle's territory will encompass the shoreline of a lake, a section of seacoast, or a stretch of a river. On Alaska's Admiralty Island and other sites where fishing is exceptionally good, well-fed bald eagles may nest less than 150 yards (137.2 m) from each other. But these cramped communities are exceptions: the average distance between nests is one or two miles (1.6–3.2 km).

An array of aggressive behaviors is employed by bald eagles with territories to defend. Mated pairs soar above their nest sites or perch in conspicuous trees and scream at intruders, broadcasting their claims to the land. Or they may physically drive away interloping eagles, circling and diving with talons extended, until the unwanted visitors retreat. Even in these situations, though, actual physical contact is extremely rare.

Building a Nest

A bald eagle's nest is nearly as impressive as its builders. The constructors of the world's largest bird nests prefer to build in the tallest trees—often over 100 feet (30.5 m), usually those with broken or deformed tops. From a nest high in a Douglas fir, Sitka spruce, western hemlock, or western redcedar, the bald eagle pair gets a good view of the surroundings. Providing plenty of room for wing flapping, the spacious, unobstructed canopy of one of these forest giants also helps the hefty birds with takeoffs and landings.

Bald eagle nests are usually located in trees near the edge of a lake, seacoast, or large river where the birds feed. Some nests, however, may be as far as a mile (1.6 km) inland. In many instances, bald eagle pairs build two, three, and even four nests in their breeding territory. The purpose of these multiple nests is unclear, but it is thought that the extra nests are intended as backups in the event that one nest is destroyed or rendered unusable. Some eagle researchers suggest that by shifting from one nest to another, year after year, the birds reduce the chances of parasite infestation. A third theory has it that bald eagles will lay eggs only after building or refurbishing a nest. Alternate nests may also serve as "no trespassing" signs, clearly establishing a pair's claim within a contested breeding territory. If a new partner is acquired, a new nest is often built.

Building on top of a previous year's nest, bald eagles can add up to 2 feet or so (.6 m) of material in a single season. They then lay their eggs on top of this forest debris. Over time, a considerable amount of material is accumulated, and the nest grows dramatically, both in size and weight. According to the *Guinness Book of World Records*, credit for the largest bird nest in the world —one that measured 9½ feet (2.9 m) across and 20 feet (6.1 m) deep—goes to a pair of bald eagles near St. Petersburg, Florida. This incredible piece of avian architecture supposedly weighed

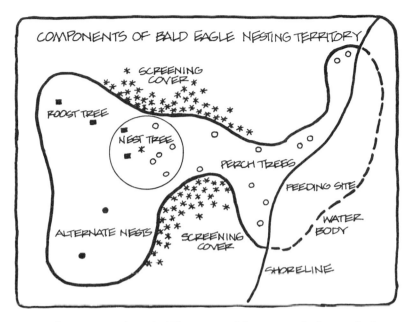

COMPONENTS OF BALD EAGLE NESTING TERRITORY

SCREENING COVER

ROOST TREE

NEST TREE

PERCH TREES

FEEDING SITE

ALTERNATE NESTS

SCREENING COVER

WATER BODY

SHORELINE

more than 2 tons (1.8 t). That record has recently been challenged by bald eagles in British Columbia, where the largest of 66 nests measured by biologists was nearly 20 feet (6.1 m) deep and growing!

Of course, the limiting factor in nest size is usually the strength of the tree that must support the mass. The shape of the tree and its branches also makes a difference. Sooner or later, most nest trees collapse under the weight of the bald eagle's nest, usually during strong winds. However, some are able to withstand the strain for remarkably long periods. A nest first seen by the members of the Lewis and Clark Expedition in 1805 is said to have endured for more than 50 years. In Alaska, the average life expectancy of a nest is about 20 years.

Nest building in the Northwest begins in January and continues through March, with both members of a pair participating in the work. A typical first-year nest is a tangle of branches, some up to 2 inches (5 cm) in diameter and 6 feet (1.8 m) in length (although most nest sticks are much smaller than this). According to some studies, eagles collect the sticks off the ground. However, eyewitnesses have reported seeing eagles use their talons to break dead branches from trees. *Craaack!*

To build a nest, bald eagles use their bills to arrange sticks in a circular, cup-shaped mass. Then, with their feet, the birds carefully arrange lighter, softer nest material—mosses, weeds, grasses, and other easily gathered plant matter—to form a lining for the middle of the nest. In coastal areas of the Northwest, this lining may also contain driftwood, bull kelp, nylon rope, eelgrass, sea lion bones, and other beach debris.

To complete their nest, the birds make a small hollow in the center, into which the eggs will be laid. The whole process of nest building may take as little time as four days or as much as several weeks. Fresh nest material is added even after the eggs have been laid; the new material may help to inhibit parasites that might otherwise attack the young. Covering the fish scales, bones, and other food waste that litter the nest may also help tidy the birds' swiftly soiled nursery.

Soon after the nest is completed, the female settles in and lays her eggs. A typical clutch contains two eggs, usually laid two to four days apart (in some instances, as much as a week). As with other raptors, incubation begins soon after the egg is laid. This causes the newborn bald eagles—called eaglets, chicks, hatchlings, or nestlings—to hatch at different times, reflecting the order in which the eggs were laid. For the next 31 to 36 days, the bald eagle pair devotes the bulk of its days and nights to keeping the eggs warm and safe.

Both male and female bald eagles incubate the eggs; however, the female usually does most of the work—nearly three-quarters of the nest duty, according to one study. To change places, one parent comes down to the nest, often from a nearby perch. Before settling down for its shift (which typically lasts one to three hours), the eagle gently probes the eggs with its beak, turning them to ensure that the warmth of incubation is evenly distributed. The eggs are in fact turned just about every hour, day and night. After it settles on the eggs, the eagle may rake nesting material around its body to seal in the warmth.

Rearing Young

If you've ever watched a chicken peck its way out of an egg, then you know that hatching is hard work. Newborn bald eagles arrive on the scene nearly blind and naked, wet, exhausted, and extremely needy. The parents have their work cut out for them.

Upon hatching, a 2½- to 3¾-ounce (70–105 g) bald eagle chick is covered with a pale gray down. Its bill is black with a whitish tip, and its skin and leg scales are vibrant pink. The newborn chick cannot regulate its body temperature, so the parents must keep it warm. For at least the first 10 days, Mom and Dad supply the heat, letting the eaglet nestle among their feathers or pulling soft, insulating nest material about the chick's body to help keep it warm.

The eaglets are watched constantly, with one parent feeding the brood, sheltering them from the elements, and keeping watch for danger—sudden winds, rainstorms, nest-robbing predators, and humans—throughout the daylight hours. For the first seven or eight weeks, the female does most of the watching and the male most of the food gathering. Four to eight feeding trips are made each day, usually in the early morning or middle to late afternoon. Such trips begin with the adult leaving its perch near the nest and performing a brief flyover, often circling high above the nest. Within half an hour, the successful hunter returns, landing on the nest to feed itself, or transferring the catch of the day to the nest tender, which then feeds the young.

Table manners are nonexistent among eaglets. The rapidly growing birds fight among themselves and beg, whine, cry, and even
scream at their parents for food. Both male and female bald eagles
feed their squabbling young, occasionally passing food between
them. Treading on the fish, fowl, or other kill, a parent breaks
the food up into chunks, then tears off bits of flesh to feed the
eaglets, bill to bill.

As the chicks grow, so do their appetites. Large nestlings can
consume nearly as much food as adults—around 2 pounds
(.9 kg) of flesh in a single meal. By the sixth or seventh week,
the eaglets are finally ready to serve themselves. They push and
shove each other, grabbing whole chunks of food away from
their parents and gobbling them down. The parents soon adjust
their feeding strategies, simply dropping off food every three or
four hours during daylight hours and letting the young ones
fend for themselves. This laissez-faire method of feeding may

continue to the day that the eaglets leave the nest and, in some instances, even after the youngsters have ostensibly set out on their own.

Because a clutch of eggs hatches over several days, a brood of three eaglets can differ in age by as much as a week. To the young bird, which can gain as much as 6 ounces (168 g) in a day, the advantage bestowed by birth order is considerable. The largest eaglet—usually the firstborn—invariably claims the most food. Much better fed, it grows at a faster rate than the rest, continuing to dominate—and often indirectly cause the death of—its second- and third-born siblings.

The whole business of battling eaglets may sound bizarre, but in matching the size of the brood to the available food resources, the nestlings' struggle to survive serves an important function. If food is abundant, more than one nestling will live to capitalize on an area's bounty. If food is scarce, perhaps only one eaglet will survive, reducing pressure on limited resources.

Mastering Flight

During their first two weeks of life, eaglets are covered with the fluffy gray down of their birth. By the third week, a second downy plumage, this one woolier and darker in hue, appears. This second batch of down is short-lived. After another week or so, the eaglet begins to sprout its true juvenile colors, a dark brown, mottled plumage that it will wear until adulthood. The new feathers grow rapidly on the back, shoulders, breast, and especially the wings. The juvenile's beak becomes a bluish black. Its talons turn black and its feet bright yellow.

Even before the first mature feathers appear, the eaglets seem to know what's in store. They flap their down-covered wings with gusto, flopping about the nest in mock flight. As their new feathers emerge, the youngsters engage in a frenzy of preening.

Downy feathers litter the nest and drift on the breeze. Eventually a coating of eagle-down "snow" covers the branches of neighboring trees and litters the ground.

In later weeks the eaglets begin to perch on the edge of their nest. They hop about and play tug-of-war with twigs and other objects. Ten to 14 weeks after hatching, they've gained most of their adult wing and tail feathers and are physically, if not psychologically, ready to leave the nest—an act, in the parlance of bird behavior, called fledging. The actual date of fledging differs from one eaglet to the next. Males are usually ready a few days before females, and single nestlings seem to fledge more rapidly than ones with nestmates.

As the time of fledging approaches, the young raptors—now nearly 95 percent of their adult size and, in many cases, weighing more than their parents—practice flying across the nest. Finally, they take their first real efforts at flight. Often these trial spins take the eaglets no farther than a neighboring tree.

Because eaglets are not always eager to set out on their own, their parents may actually coerce them to fly. Adult eagles have been seen using food as a lure and taunting their reluctant offspring with wing flaps and vocalizations, with the apparent hope of motivating the youngsters to leave the nest.

Lacking the strength and coordination of their parents, most immature eagles are awkward fliers at first. Crash landings are commonplace, especially when these novices try to perch on tree limbs. Large numbers—perhaps as many as half the fledglings—invariably ground themselves after their first flights. Because the ground cover beneath nest trees can be dense, the young eagles may experience great difficulty in taking off again. On the ground, they risk starvation or falling prey to bears and other large animals of the forest.

For the first four to six weeks after fledging, the young eagles remain attached to the nest site and to their parents—seldom straying more than half a mile (.8 km) from the nest. While many continue to receive food from the parents, they may also begin to forage on their own. More independent birds even follow their parents on hunting trips, refining their flying skills and landing techniques along the way.

Seven weeks after fledging, most young can still be found within a mile (1.6 km) of their nests. Over the next few weeks, however, they lose their attachment to home and begin to wander, often led by appetite and the prevailing winds. Eight to 10 weeks after fledging, a stronger instinct to move develops. They may embark on their first migration, eventually returning to the general area of their birth. Or they may move to areas where prey is abundant, joining the adult bald eagles in hunting, scavenging, and stealing food.

Immature eagles have a wing-and-tail-to-body ratio that is proportionately larger than the ratio for adults, making the immatures better adapted for soaring. As the birds molt each year, the feathers are replaced with progressively shorter ones. Riding the wind's thermals and updrafts, immature eagles scan the horizon for spiraling columns of soaring adult eagles—clues, visible at a distance of 15 or more miles (24 km), that could lead them to a source of carrion. Adult bald eagles can flap their comparatively shorter wings at faster rates than immature eagles. Capable of covering up to 32 miles (51.2 km) in an hour, they are more efficient than their young at chasing down and dispatching live prey.

Finding Food

An adult bald eagle is a well-equipped predator. Its massive wingspan, sharp hawk's beak, and tigerlike talons are exquisitely adapted to meting out death from above.

Like other birds of prey, bald eagles have a lightweight body, muscular wings, and a broad tail adapted for maneuverability and precision in the air. The eagle's hollow bones weigh less than half the total weight of its feathers, and its wingspan, which approaches 8 feet (2.4 m) in adult females, is ideal for catching thermals—the upwardly moving masses of warm air created by the sun as it heats the earth.

Rising higher and higher on the thermals, a bald eagle can gain altitude until it is a mere speck in the sky. Here it soars and glides, conserving energy as it patiently waits and watches for the opportunity to swoop down and make a kill. Special feathers (called alulae) attached to the remnant "thumb" of the wing operate like the slots of an airplane's wing. These short feathers can be adjusted by the eagle to reduce turbulence, which in turn increases the bird's maneuverability and its ability to maintain a steady flight pattern. Further maneuverability is imparted by the eagle's tail feathers, which can be tilted or spread, serving the same function as the rudder and elevators of an airplane when turning, slowing, or stabilizing in midflight.

As with most birds of prey, a bald eagle's vision is remarkably acute. The eye of an eagle is actually larger than a human's, with resolving power (the ability to distinguish details at a distance) three or four times greater than our own. And, because the position of their eyes allows a degree of binocular vision, bald eagles can perceive depth—a crucial ability, especially when diving at prey. The lens of the eye is extremely soft, allowing for rapid changes in near and far accommodation (focusing).

The bald eagle's exceptionally large, muscular feet are additional aids to hunting. Measured along its curvature, the hallux, or hind claw, of an eagle can be 3 inches (7.5 cm) long. At the moment of contact with a fish, bird, or mammal, the tendons of the eagle's leg flex, automatically drawing the toes tightly together. The needle-sharp hallux and the three other talons of the eagle's foot are drawn toward each other to penetrate the skin and muscle—and occasionally the bone—of the prey. Tiny spikes called spicules on the bottoms of the toes aid in gripping slippery fish. Barely wetting its talons, a bald eagle can skim the surface of a body of water, snatch a fish, and carry it up into the air.

In southeast Alaska, eagles have been observed flying low over the ocean, ambushing unsuspecting seabirds by hiding in the troughs of ocean swells. Once an eagle has singled out a victim, it gives chase until its prey is exhausted. If the clarity of water permits, an eagle may circle above, watching waterfowl try to elude this single-minded predator by swimming underwater. Occasionally, two or more eagles will hunt cooperatively, with one flushing rabbits or ducks from cover and the others closing in for the kill.

While hunting plays an important part in a bald eagle's life, especially among adults, robbing other birds and scavenging on carrion are also frequently practiced means of getting food. This by no means makes the bald eagle a less worthy bird of prey: the flexible feeding strategy—hunting, stealing, and scavenging—allows the eagle to conserve energy while capitalizing on whatever food is available.

Benjamin Franklin, who preferred the wild turkey for the symbol of our nation, wrote of the bald eagle, "He is a bird of bad moral character. He does not get his living honestly." In a way, Franklin was right: bald eagles are born thieves. As nestlings they snatch morsels away from each other. As subadults, they tussle over larger scraps of flesh, sometimes stealing meals from their elders. Adults tear whole fish and waterfowl from the beaks and talons of hawks, ospreys, and other raptors. Occasionally, several eagles team up to make a winged hunter—often a fish-nabbing osprey in flight —drop its catch.

In addition to catching its own prey or stealing food, the bald eagle will feed on carrion. This is especially true in winter, when many of the major rivers of the Northwest are filled with the carcasses of spent spawning salmon, washed onto gravel bars or into water shallow enough for the eagles to wade in. Where the fish runs are large, and late in the year—as they are on Alaska's Chilkat River or the Skagit River in Washington—and the conditions right, bald eagles have a feast. Crows and gulls frequently join them to dine on the dead. However, it's the eagles who gobble up over 90 percent of the salmon littering the banks.

Farther inland, away from the salmon runs, bald eagles feed on the carcasses of deer, elk, and other large mammals that have died during unusually cold winters. Throughout history, farmers and ranchers have misinterpreted the eagle's habit of feeding on the remains of pigs, sheep, cows, and other livestock. The misguided impulse of these people to save their animals from "marauding" bald eagles led to the placing of bounties on these birds.

Eagle Behavior

SOARING Aerial displays such as soaring (long, gliding flight aided by thermals) and chasing often occur in the late morning and continue through the afternoon during spring and winter months. Chases and dives among several bald eagles or between a pair of birds are often observed, and these behaviors are believed to be associated with courtship.

TALON DISPLAY "Taloning"—the brief locking of two bald eagles' claws—is an activity frequently practiced by two immature eagles, by an immature eagle and an adult, or by two adults. While soaring, one bird suddenly dives at another, and the attacked individual rolls over at the last minute, displaying its talons to the attacker. Sometimes the talons of the two eagles will link briefly, causing both birds to spiral dramatically downward. Taloning also occurs during food disputes between bald eagles and other birds of prey.

WING DISPLAYS Wing movements are part of a bald eagle's body language. During food squabbles, a bald eagle may raise its outstretched wings

in a threatening gesture, or it may drape them around its food, protecting a contested morsel with a behavioral pose called "mantling." While perching in a tree, a bald eagle often unfolds and extends its wings in an activity known as "sunning," to take full advantage of the sun's warming rays.

ROOSTING During harsh winter months, eagles are very careful to conserve their energy. They may spend nearly three-quarters of their time in the roost, and will leave it only during daylight. Generally, the eagles leave their roost just before sunrise, returning after feeding, usually in the early afternoon. Where eagles congregate in large numbers, it's not uncommon to see several hundred of them occupying a single stand of trees. Scientists call this "communal roosting," a behavior that may lead to the formation of pair-bonds or serve to bring birds together prior to long-distance flights. Don't assume, however, that the birds are always happy to roost en masse. They jostle each other while squabbling over favored perches, and scream when a new bird arrives to join the group.

BILLING Before mating and building a nest, a member of a bald eagle pair perches next to its mate, pecking lightly at its beak in a behavior commonly called "billing." Pairs also preen the feathers of each other's head, neck, back, or breast.

VOCALIZATIONS Although bald eagles have several distinct, raucous calls, many of which can be heard for long distances, we can only guess at their actual purposes. The birds are particularly vocal in communal roosting areas and while feeding in groups. Individual birds also vocalize, perhaps as a warning, when intruders threaten their nest or enter their territory. In addition, bald eagles vocalize during courtship. Eaglets appear to have a language all their own—everything from a quiet *yeep* to a shrill scream—for signaling their needs.

Back from the Brink

Since Colonial times, when hundreds of thousands of eagles soared in our skies, the number of bald eagles in North America has dramatically declined. A report from 1668 states that many of an "infinite number" of wintering eagles at Casco Bay, Maine, were shot and fed to hogs. Population in the contiguous 48 states reached an all-time low—quite possibly as few as 3,700 individuals—in the early 1960s, a full decade after the first formal measures were taken to assure the bald eagle's continued existence.

Long regarded as vermin by farmers and ranchers, the birds became targets for bounty hunters in Alaska, who, as recently as 1962, were paid two dollars by the state for every pair of bald eagle feet they brought in. Even more recently, ranchers in Wyoming paid helicopter pilots and gunners 25 dollars for every eagle they could kill.

The hunting of bald eagles didn't end with the dissolution of bounty programs. Arrests and convictions of suppliers and buyers of bald eagle feathers continue to occur. In 1980, an estimated 75 bald eagles were killed for their feathers (which are in demand as decoration) along the delta of Washington's Nooksack River. Bald eagle rehabilitation centers in the United States and Canada regularly receive birds with gunshot wounds—indications of the need for continual public education about eagles and other large birds of prey.

Clearly, actions by ill-informed humans have contributed to the vast majority of bald eagle deaths. For example, the birds have been robbed of habitat through the clearing of forests by loggers and developers. Breeding pairs require healthy old-growth trees that can support the weight of their nests. By cutting these trees, we have eliminated many potential nest sites. Along with their habitat, the food base of the birds has been reduced, as historically large runs of salmon have been diverted by dams or destroyed through overfishing throughout the Northwest.

Bald eagles also have been poisoned with agricultural pesticides —especially the now-outlawed chemical compound DDT, which weakens the shells of the birds' eggs. Eagles have been electrocuted while perching on power lines and fatally mangled in collisions with buildings and automobiles.

Formal protection of the bald eagle began with the passage of the federal Bald Eagle Protection Act (now the Eagle Protection Act) of 1940, a measure that provides for fines of up to $10,000 and two years' imprisonment for people who harm bald and golden eagles. Efforts at protection were stepped up substantially in 1973 with the passage of the federal Endangered Species Act, which increased the penalties for molesting eagles. This second act requires managers of federal lands to prepare recovery plans for listed species of animals and plants. Subsequent federal and state laws have mandated that bald eagle nesting and roosting habitats be managed to maintain and increase eagle numbers to the point of recovery—the threshold where bald eagle populations can sustain themselves and thus be no longer classified as threatened or endangered. To achieve these goals, five regional bald eagle recovery teams were appointed by the U.S. secretary of the interior.

The Pacific States Bald Eagle Recovery Team, established in 1979, was charged with drafting a management plan for bald eagle habitats in Washington, Oregon, Idaho, Montana, California, Wyoming, and Nevada. In 1986, when the team's plan was approved, bald eagles were classified as threatened in Washington and Oregon and endangered in the other five states. Only in Alaska and Canada—areas outside the team's scope— were the birds considered abundant.

By 1990, the team determined that the bald eagle population in the Northwest had increased to 861 nesting pairs—nearly triple the number tallied in 1980. "It is difficult," notes the 1990 report, "to think of the bald eagle as still being on 'the brink of extinction' in the West." Based on population data from 1986–1990, team members now agree that the five states' "endangered" eagles can now be upgraded to "threatened."

Team members, however, are not entirely optimistic about the future of bald eagles in the Northwest, and many believe that the trend toward recovery may one day reverse itself. They cite the eagles' uneven geographic distribution, the very low reproductive rates of some populations (for example, those of the lower Columbia River, where high concentrations of pesticides and other pollutants have been found in eggs), and dwindling habitat. Changing the eagles' listing from endangered to threatened (or removing them from the Endangered Species list) could foster the false impression that the birds have recovered fully and no longer need individual or habitat protection.

If humans and bald eagles are to coexist, steps must be taken to address all of these concerns. Information on what you can do to help protect bald eagles can be obtained from any of the sources cited at the end of this book.

Sometimes It's Best to Leave Bald Eagles Alone

Unlike their relative the osprey, which can feed and breed even when humans are present, bald eagles need a high degree of isolation from people to effectively perform these functions. Eagles that are building nests, incubating eggs, and rearing their young are strongly deterred by human activity. If people approach too near a bald eagle nest, the parents may abandon their eggs or, after the eggs hatch, refrain from feeding or warming the nestlings.

The Washington State Department of Wildlife recommends that a circle of undisturbed habitat 330 feet (99 m) in diameter be maintained throughout the year to preserve a bald eagle nest site, and that the diameter of this area be doubled when the birds are breeding. Most considerate bird-watchers go even further, refraining from approaching within a quarter-mile (.4 km) of a known bald eagle nest. Under these conditions, a high-powered pair of binoculars or a spotter's scope (a monocular viewing instrument available at some sporting goods outlets) is an essential tool for eagle-watching.

Care must also be taken when watching bald eagles during nonbreeding times. In areas where the birds congregate during winter months, the appearance of people may unintentionally prevent them from feeding on carcasses of salmon or other carrion. Eagles waste valuable time and energy fleeing human intruders; and, if they are continually prevented from feeding, some may eventually starve to death. In some instances, wintering eagles become accustomed to visitors. However, those that can't adjust may be forced to flee to habitats where food resources are scarce.

By joining other participants in programs offered by the National Audubon Society and its local chapters, the Nature Conservancy, or a reputable independent charter operation, eagle-watchers can limit their effects on wintering birds. A single, carefully planned visit by a large group of people is much less likely to disturb feeding patterns than a steady stream of unescorted individuals.

BALD EAGLES NEED:
- A reliable source of salmon or other high-protein food
- Free-flowing water
- Tall trees for nest sites and for viewing potential prey
- Privacy for nesting, feeding, and rearing young

EAGLE-WATCHERS NEED:
- Binoculars or other devices for long-distance viewing
- Warm, waterproof clothing
- Sensitivity to surroundings
- Patience

Watching Bald Eagles: Spring, Summer, and Early Autumn

With the arrival of warm weather, adult and immature bald eagles can be seen throughout southeast Alaska, soaring in large numbers, perching in trees, and feeding on herring and other small schooling fish near shore. The same behavior can be seen from March through August throughout coastal British Columbia, where an estimated 4,000 breeding pairs are thought to exist. Many of these birds return to nest sites after wintering in Washington and along the coast of Alaska.

In Washington, where an estimated 400 breeding pairs can be found, summer eagles are best seen on the forested coast of the Olympic Peninsula and in the somewhat isolated sanctuaries of the San Juan Islands. Some bald eagles even return to nest sites in urban areas, such as Seattle's Discovery Park. Approximately 200 bald eagle pairs nest in Oregon—most along the upper Deschutes River in the Willamette National Forest. The majority of Idaho and Montana's birds are migratory. Bird-watchers report close to 100 nesting pairs in Montana. Soaring eagles are commonly seen by motorists along Interstate Highway 90, which parallels the Yellowstone River between Bozeman and Billings.

It's important to remember that spring and summer are when bald eagle pairs are building nests, laying eggs, and rearing their young. Utmost care must be taken not to disturb them at these times. In general, the best viewing points are elevated areas— hills, bridges, ships' decks—at distances of at least 1,000 yards (.9 km). These place the observer at the same level as the eagles' treetop homes. Because bald eagles are more tolerant of intruders approaching by water routes, charter fishing or nature cruise boats provide the most environmentally sound observation. Large commercial cruise ships plying the waters of the Queen Charlotte Islands, the Inside Passage, or other eagle haunts in summer also offer excellent opportunities for low-impact viewing. The crews of many of these floating hotels include professional naturalists specially trained to assist passengers in sighting and identifying resident birds and mammals. Fine opportunities are also afforded riders of Washington, Alaska, and Canada ferries.

Watching Bald Eagles:
Late Autumn and Winter

As autumn draws to a close and winter begins, many eagles move southward from Alaska and British Columbia. Where food is most abundant and the weather less severe, they huddle together, sharing resources in seasonal congregations that can contain fewer than a dozen or more than a thousand birds. Such impressive winter congregations offer the best opportunities for viewing eagles up close. In many areas, the birds have adapted well to the frequent presence of people.

For photographing wintering bald eagles, a telephoto lens of 400 mm or more will greatly increase the chances of taking a successful picture. **Remember at all times that the welfare of the eagle is more important than getting a good picture.** Photos should only be taken when conditions are right.

The largest seasonal gathering of eagles anywhere in the world occurs on the Chilkat River flats, just outside of Haines, in southern Alaska. To protect the birds from harassment, the state of Alaska recently created a preserve out of the 49,000 acres surrounding the flats. During peak salmon spawning season, in November, as many as 3,500 immature and adult bald eagles have been known to gather here.

British Columbia's 1988 midwinter survey tallied 8,400 bald eagles, of which nearly three-quarters resided in southern coastal areas. Nearly 2 percent of these—mostly immature bald eagles—were spotted scavenging in the garbage dumps of the province's larger settlements. North of Vancouver, an average of 2,000 eagles congregate along the Squamish River to feed on the carcasses of spawned-out salmon.

Along the Skagit River, in Washington, as many as 400 birds feed on leftovers from the river's healthy chum salmon run. Float trips sponsored by conservation organizations and private tour groups bring hundreds of people to the Skagit every year. Most of these tours are scheduled for midmorning or early afternoon—times when the eagles are roosting and sunbathing —so that the eagles' chances of feeding are not reduced. Designated viewing areas and off-limits sanctuaries have been established to allow the birds the privacy they need.

Food sources diminish and the number of eagles decreases south of Washington and away from the coast. In Oregon, the biggest winter gathering of bald eagles takes place in the Lower Klamath Basin, where as many as a thousand migratory birds assemble from November to March. As many as 200 eagles also winter on the lower Columbia between Portland and Astoria, Oregon. Protection afforded by Yellowstone, the first national park in the United States, has helped eagle populations rebound in neighboring Montana and Idaho. Near Canyon Ferry Village, 20 miles (32 km) northeast of Helena, Montana, more than 250 eagles feed on the remains of kokanee salmon during peak viewing season—from mid-November to mid-December—along the Missouri River. While the winter population of northern Idaho's Lake Pend Oreille approaches 400 birds, most of the state's winter bald eagle congregations usually consist of less than 50.

Guide to Listings

Listings are arranged geographically, by state and province. Each listing is numbered for easy location on the accompanying map. Each contains a description of the eagle-watching location, viewing tips, and other pertinent information.

Only those sites that can be visited without interrupting the eagles' breeding or feeding activities have been included in this guide. For a complete, up-to-date list of bald eagle tour guides and excursion operators, including addresses and phone numbers, send a stamped, self-addressed envelope to:

SASQUATCH BOOKS
1008 Western Avenue, Ste. 300
Seattle, WA 98104

In lieu of this list, the following suggestions should prove helpful in locating the best viewing areas:

1. In smaller towns, contact the tourist information center or a recreational equipment supplier.

2. In larger cities, consult the Yellow Pages (likely categories include Environmental Associations, Museums, Tour Operators, and Tourist Information) or contact the city zoo, aquarium, or museum. A phone call to the biology department of the local college or university may also produce results.

Surveys of bald eagle populations are conducted annually by wildlife biologists in several northwestern states. If you spot a bald eagle nest or eagles with markers on their wings or legs, or have other information that could be helpful to the surveys, record the information carefully and contact the appropriate agency or organization as listed at the end of this book.

A final note: Should you know of good eagle-watching sites not identified in this book, we'd like to hear from you. Send your tips to Sasquatch Books.

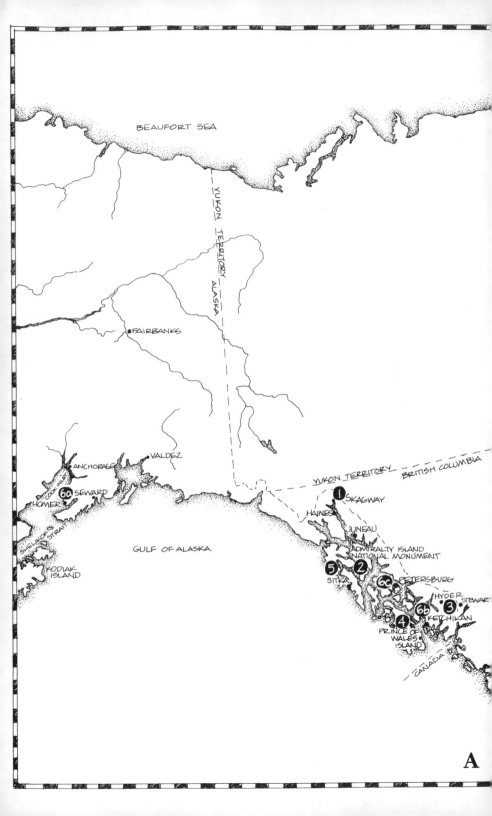

Alaska *(see map A)*

1. CHILKAT BALD EAGLE PRESERVE Near Haines, where warm-water upwellings keep the Chilkat River from freezing, as many as 3,500 eagles gather to feed on chum salmon. Peak months are October through December.

   Best viewing: By car or tour bus, 18–22 miles (28.8–35.2 km) north of Haines on Haines Highway, at designated roadside pullouts; by charter raft excursion from mid-May to mid-September.

   Information: Haines Visitor Center
   Haines Chamber of Commerce
   Box 530
   Haines, AK 99827   (907) 766-2234, or (800) 458-3579

2. ADMIRALTY ISLAND NATIONAL MONUMENT Part of Tongass National Forest, Admiralty Island boasts the highest density of bald eagle nests in North America. Best viewing (at a distance) is from April to August.

   Best viewing: By floatplane from Juneau or Sitka; by private boat or Alaska Marine Highway System ferry, which stops at Angoon on the island. Cabins by reservation, shelters and campsites on a first-come, first-served basis.

   Information: U.S. Forest Service
   Centennial Hall
   101 Egan Drive
   Juneau, AK 99801   (907) 586-8751

3. MISTY FJORDS NATIONAL MONUMENT Also part of Tongass National Forest, another area rich in eagle nest sites.

   Best viewing: The monument is accessible by floatplane from Ketchikan or by car from Stewart, B.C., on Highway 37. There are several rustic cabins for rent in the vicinity.

4. PRINCE OF WALES ISLAND Good eagle-watching in spring and summer via unpaved roads at Sandy Beach, Thorne Bay, and Thorne River Estuary.

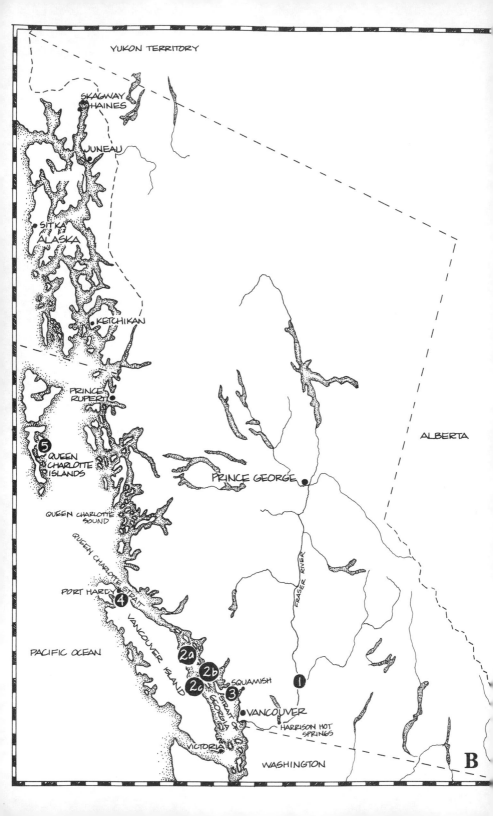

Best viewing: Accessible by ferry from Ketchikan to the town of Hollis on the island.

5. SITKA Home of the Alaska Raptor Rehabilitation Center. The center treats injured eagles, releasing them into the wild when possible. Birds with injuries that prevent them from returning to the wild are kept for purposes of further study. Talks on bald eagle natural history are timed to coincide with tour vessel arrivals; the center also serves independent travelers who give prior notice.

Best viewing: Accessible by air from Juneau or Anchorage, by tour vessel, or by Alaska Marine Highway System ferry.

6a, 6b, 6c. HOMER, KETCHIKAN, PETERSBURG Eagles congregate during fish-processing season (spring and summer).

Access: By air from Anchorage or Alaska Marine Highway System ferry.

British Columbia (see map B)

1. CHEHALIS FLATS Between 300 and 400 birds gather from November through February at the confluence of the Fraser and Lower Harrison rivers. Best viewing is on foot and by automobile, upstream from Harrison Mills on Highway 7 and in Kilby Provincial Park.

2. VANCOUVER ISLAND Campbell River (2a), the self-proclaimed "Salmon Capital of the World," hosts more than 100 overwintering bald eagles each year. Many of these birds remain in the area in spring and summer, nesting in the coniferous trees that line the shores outside of town and on nearby Quadra Island. Other eagle-watching hot spots include Gabriola Island (2b) and the Qualicum River (2c) downstream of the fish hatchery, and the coastline between Comox and Courtenay.

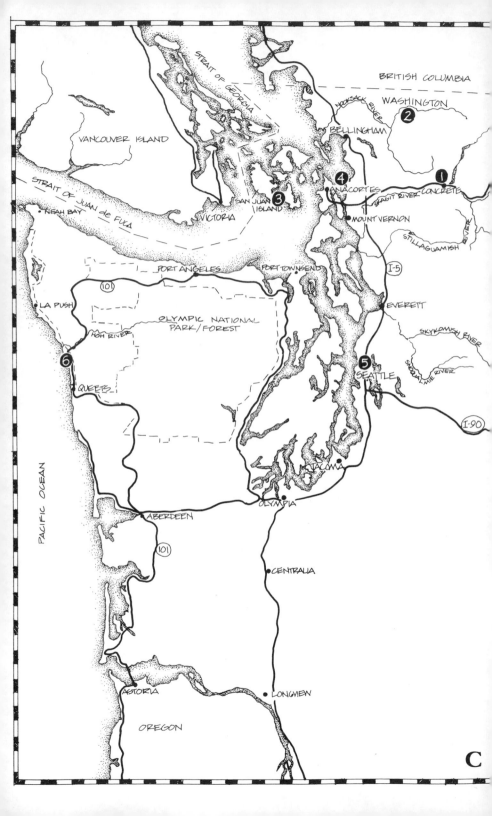

3. SQUAMISH RIVER Along the Squamish River, outside the
   towns of Squamish and Brackendale, are important overwintering areas for around 200 adult bald eagles. In exceptionally good years as many as 600 adult bald eagles have
   been counted at these two locales.

4. PORT HARDY TO PRINCE RUPERT The popular Inside
   Passage route of the BC Ferries (a 15- to 20-hour trip)
   puts you at eye level with nesting and roosting bald eagles.
   At just about any time of year, you're almost guaranteed a
   dozen or more eagle sightings.

5. QUEEN CHARLOTTE ISLANDS Bald eagles can be seen
   here year round, especially at Cape St. James, where local
   bird-watchers have tallied as many as 500 bald eagles in a
   season. Eagle-watching by charter boat is generally limited
   by weather to spring and summer months.

Washington (see map C)

1. SKAGIT RIVER BALD EAGLE NATIONAL AREA Between
   400 and 500 bald eagles gather from November to early
   March to feed on spawning chum salmon. Peak time is
   December 20 to January 30.

   Best viewing: By car on State Highway 20 between
   Rockport and Marblemount, at designated roadside pull-
   outs on Rockport Bridge (near Howard Miller Steelhead
   Park); by charter raft excursion.

   ** Special event: Annual Bald Eagle Festival, usually
   held on the first weekend in February in Skagit County.
   Call the Mount Baker ranger station for location and
   schedule of events; (206) 856-5700.

   Contact:
   U.S. Forest Service, Mount Baker Ranger Station
   2105 Highway 20, Sedro Woolley, WA; 98284
   (206) 856-5700

2. NOOKSACK RIVER As many as 150 wintering eagles gather in January and February, east of Bellingham, between Deming and Maple Falls.

   Best viewing: By car at Welcome Bridge, ½ mile (.8 km) east of State Highway 542 on Mosquito Lake Road.

3. SAN JUAN ISLANDS Highest density of bald eagle nests in the state, best viewed at a distance from January through August. Public access at Cattle Point (American Camp), on San Juan Island.

   Best viewing: From Washington State ferry; by private boat or by charter nature cruise from Friday Harbor.

4. PADILLA BAY NATIONAL ESTUARINE RESERVE In spring and summer months, bald eagles can be seen along the protected shoreline of this teeming estuary outside of Anacortes.

   Best viewing: By car, ¼ mile (.4 km) north of Bay View State Park, then on foot. Inquire at interpretive center (open Wednesday–Sunday) for current eagle observation areas and for scheduled programs on eagle ecology. Beach trail is closed on Mondays.

5. DISCOVERY PARK, SEATTLE A breeding pair of bald eagles returns to Magnolia Bluff in late February and remains until July; best times for viewing are in mid-May, when eaglets have fledged.

   Best viewing: Inquire at visitor center (open daily), the staff of which gives periodic presentations on eagles.

6. OLYMPIC NATIONAL PARK Nest sites and wintering areas are spread out across the park lands. Eagles are easy to spot at coastal beaches #2 and #3 near La Push.

   Best viewing: On foot, from hiking trails.

7. FRANKLIN ROOSEVELT LAKE (shown on page 42) Over 200 wintering eagles gather behind Grand Coulee Dam and at nearby Banks Lake from November through March.

Best viewing: By car, along Highway 25 on the east side of lake from Kettle Falls south to town of Hunters.

Oregon *(see map D)*

1. SAUVIE ISLAND BAR Wintering eagles, up to 40 per day from November to March, congregate here between the Willamette and Columbia rivers.

   Best viewing: By car and on foot. Reserve is open until dark, seven days a week. Maps are available at the Oregon Department of Fish and Game office at the Game Management Area, approximately 2 miles (3.2 km) west of Lynton on State Highway 30.

2. KNAPPA Between 15 and 20 wintering eagles gather to feed on the mud flats at Twilight Eagle Sanctuary, a privately developed eagle-watching site, from the end of November into May.

   Best viewing: By car, from State Highway 30, 12 miles (19.2 km) east of Astoria, to Knappa, following signs to Burnside on the Columbia River.

3. FORT ROCK VALLEY From late January through March, 40 to 50 wintering eagles feed on waterfowl and deer carrion at this protected area south of Bend, between Fort Rock and Silver Lake.

   Best viewing: By car and on foot. Obtain updated information from the U.S. Forest Service office in Bend.

4. UPPER CROOKED RIVER (EAST OF PRINEVILLE NEAR PAULINA) As many as 60 wintering eagles gather from late January through March to feed on waterfowl and deer carrion.

5. LOWER KLAMATH BASIN (ALSO INCLUDES LOWER KLAMATH LAKE AND TULE LAKE IN NORTHEAST CALIFORNIA) Oregon's most populated wintering area attracts

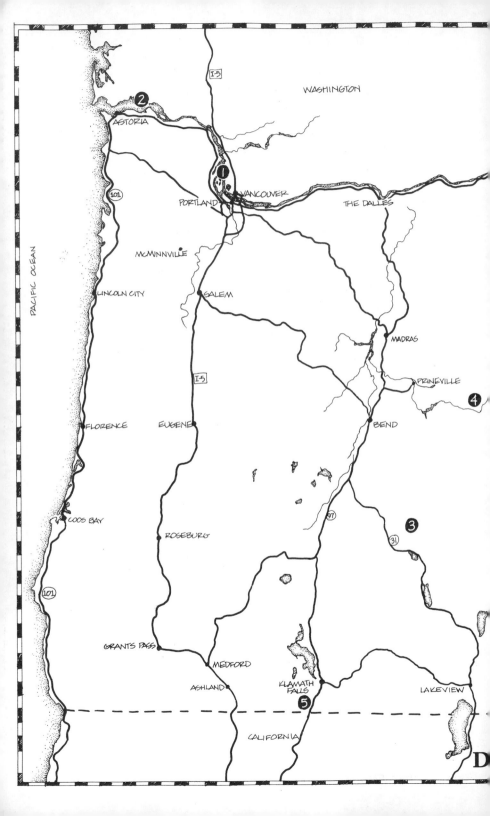

600 to 1,000 eagles from November to March. Peak times are late January and February. Nests of as many as four dozen breeding pairs can also be found here.

Best viewing: By car, along self-guided tour route on the Lower Klamath National Wildlife Refuge and on foot at Bear Valley National Wildlife Refuge on Highway 97. Inquire at the Oregon Department of Fish and Wildlife office in Klamath Falls.

** Special event: Annual Klamath Basin Bald Eagle Conference in February.

Contact: Klamath Basin Audubon Society
P.O. Box 354
Klamath Falls, OR 97601

Idaho (see map E)

1. LAKE COEUR D'ALENE As many as 40 wintering eagles congregate on the shores of this 25-mile-long (40 km) lake from late November to the end of January.

   Best viewing: At Wolf Bay Lodge and at Beauty Bay, both on State Highway 95 on the west side of the lake.

2. LAKE PEND OREILLE Up to 400 birds can be seen in the vicinity of the lake, feeding on carcasses of spawning kokanee salmon, from early November through mid-February. Numbers peak around Christmas.

   Best viewing: By car from the bridge over Pend Oreille River, approximately 44 miles (70.4 km) north of Coeur d'Alene on State Highway 95; other viewing spots accessible by car at the north end of the lake; on the east side of the lake at the mouth of the Clark Fork River.

3. KOOTENAI RIVER Along State Highway 2 near the Idaho-Montana border.

4. DEER FLAT NATIONAL WILDLIFE REFUGE As many as 40 wintering eagles feed on the shores of Lake Lowell

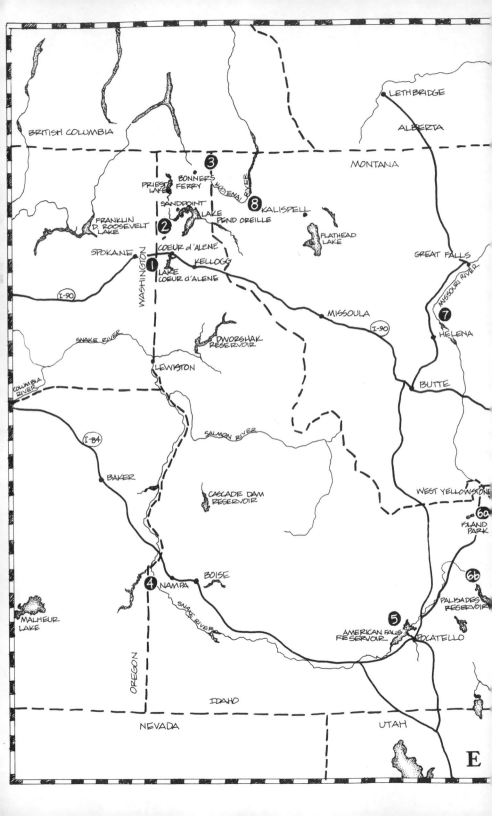

E

(west of Nampa, near Boise) from mid-October
to January.

Best viewing: Inside the refuge headquarters building,
between 8 and 9:30 A.M.

5. AMERICAN FALLS RESERVOIR An area seasonally rich in
waterfowl—around 20,000 ducks and another 20,000
geese gather here—supports a healthy population of about
50 wintering eagles.

Best viewing: On foot, from the north side of the reservoir, near the town of Springfield; on the south side from
the Fort Hall Indian Reservation. Request a trespassing
permit from the Shoshone-Bannock tribes at P.O. Box
306, Fort Hall, ID 83203.

6a, 6b. TARGHEE NATIONAL FOREST More than 60 eagles
spend the winter in Targhee National Forest, due west
of Yellowstone National Park. A record number—100
individuals—was tallied by eagle-watchers in the winter
of 1990–91.

Best viewing: At Island Park Reservoir, northeast of
Idaho Falls on State Highway 20, near Harriman State
Park; along the south fork of the Snake River, especially at
Palisades Reservoir, along State Highway 26, 15–18 miles
(24–28.8 km) from the Wyoming border.

Montana (see map E)

7. HAUSER LAKE Over 250 migrating eagles have tradition-
ally gathered from mid-November to mid-December
along the Missouri River near Helena. In recent years as
many as 400 birds have been seen here.

Best viewing: By car, north of Canyon Ferry Dam on
Canyon Ferry Road east from Interstate Highway 15. The
visitor information center maintains several interpretive

displays on eagles during peak viewing season. Other fine sites are at nearby Beaver Creek (in Helena National Forest), the York Bridge Fishing Access, and Riverside Campgrounds at Canyon Ferry State Park.

8. KOOTENAI RIVER Below Libby Dam (which forms Lake Koocanusa in Kootenai National Forest), as many as 40 eagles a day can be observed during the fall migration—from mid-October to mid-December. Typically in January and February, between 15 and 25 wintering eagles can also be counted. In 1989, a record 200 wintering eagles were tallied. Nests of 15 breeding pairs have also been found at this site.

9. FORT PECK DAM (not shown) The reservoir behind the dam has gradually gained in popularity with wintering bald eagles, which feed on cisco, a variety of whitefish introduced to the area several years ago. Forty-three wintering birds were counted in 1989, more than four times the number seen in previous years.

Best viewing: At designated viewing areas constructed by the U.S. Army Corps of Engineers.

** Note: Report sightings of eagles with markers on wings or legs to the Montana Department of Fish, Wildlife and Parks, 1404 8th Avenue, Helena, MT 59620; (406) 444-4720.

Information Sources

ALASKA

Alaska Raptor Rehabilitation Center
P.O. Box 2984
1101 Sawmill Creek Road
Sitka, AK 99835

National Audubon Society
308 G Street, Suite 217
Anchorage, AK 99501

BRITISH COLUMBIA

Federation of B.C. Naturalists
Room 321
1361 W. Broadway
Vancouver, B.C. V6H 4A9

WASHINGTON

Eagle Rehabilitation Program
Woodland Park Zoological Gardens
5500 Phinney Avenue N.
Seattle, WA 98103

Nongame Program
Washington State Department of
    Wildlife
600 N. Capitol Way
Olympia, WA 98501-1090

Washington Field Office
The Nature Conservancy
217 Pine Street, Suite 1100
Seattle, WA 98101

Washington State Office
National Audubon Society
P.O. Box 462
Olympia, WA 98507

OREGON

National Audubon Society
555 Audubon Place
Sacramento, CA 95825

Oregon Department of Fish and
    Wildlife
4343 Miller Island Road
Klamath Falls, OR 97601

Oregon Field Office
The Nature Conservancy
821 SE 14th Avenue
Portland, OR 97214

IDAHO

National Audubon Society
4150 Darley, Suite 5
Boulder, CO 80303

Raptor Research and Technical
    Assistance Center
Bureau of Land Management
3948 Development Avenue
Boise, ID 83705

MONTANA

Montana Department of Fish, Wildlife
    and Parks
1420 E. Sixth Avenue
Helena, MT 59620

National Audubon Society
4150 Darley, Suite 5
Boulder, CO 80303

To Learn More About Eagles

BOOKS:

Jon M. Gerrard and Gary R. Bortolotti, *The Bald Eagle: Haunts and Habits of a Wilderness Monarch* (Washington, D.C.: Smithsonian Institution Press, 1988)

Tom and Pat Leeson, *The American Eagle* (Hillsboro, Ore.: Beyond Words Publishing Inc., 1988)

Mark Stalmaster, *The Bald Eagle* (New York: Universe Books, 1987)

Donald W. Stokes, *A Guide to Bird Behavior*, Vol. III (Boston: Little, Brown and Company, 1989)

John K. Terres, *The Audubon Society Encyclopedia of North American Birds* (New York: Alfred A. Knopf Inc., 1980)

VIDEOTAPE:

Peter Roberts, *Eagles* (Seattle: Peter Roberts Productions, 1989; approximately 40 minutes)